*Dedicated to the best of all creation,
Sayyidina Muhammad* ﷺ

and to Dawud and Adam

© Copyright 2021 Halima Publishing

All rights reserved. Apart from personal or study use, no part of this book may be copied or reproduced, stored in a retrieval system, or transmitted in any form or by any means, electronic, electrical, chemical, mechanical, optical, photocopying, recording or otherwise, without the prior permission of the copyright owner.

ISBN 9781999802752

Halima Publishing
Hambleden, Buckinghamshire, U.K.
www.halimapublishing.co.uk

Adapted by Yasmin Watson
Illustrations by Hana Horack-Elyafi
Copy edititing by Lisa Edwards

Stories from the Battles of the Prophet Muhammad ﷺ

Adapted by Yasmin Watson

Illustrated by Hana Horack-Elyafi

Stories from the Battles of the Prophet Muhammad

Adapted by Yasmin Wahba

Illustrated by Tana Hoban-Dyah

Contents

Foreword	VII
Prologue	XI
Battle of Badr	1
Battle of Uhud	19
Battle of the Trench	45
Conquest of Makkah	65
Rules of Battle in Islam	91
Notes	94
Symbols and Translations	96
References and Further Reading	98

STORIES FROM THE BATTLES OF THE PROPHET MUHAMMAD

Foreword

In seventh-century Arabia, justice was thin on the ground - there was no government or police. The only people of authority were tribe leaders, but they only protected people of their own tribe and many were known for their arrogance, conceit, and vindictiveness. Blood feuds would last for generations.

Muhammad ﷺ was born into the Banu Hashim family, part of the Quraysh, one of the largest and most powerful tribes of Makkah. He was a popular and respected person and given the title '*Al-Amin*': 'The Trustworthy'. When he was forty years old, he began to receive revelations of the Qur'an and he started preaching about the new religion of Islam with its messages of peace, unity and faith in One God. But the Quraysh felt uneasy.

The Quraysh saw Islam as a threat to their very way of being because idol worship had been established for hundreds of years. People often resist change and none more so than the Quraysh of Makkah. The Muslims were mercilessly persecuted by the Quraysh, some of them being tortured or even killed.

Many of the people of Makkah had a passionate hatred of the new religion, especially Abu Jahl and Abu Lahab, who wanted to kill the Prophet ﷺ. If it wasn't for the protection of Abu Talib, the Prophet's ﷺ Uncle, he would not have been able to remain in Makkah for as long as he did, such was the threat on his life.

The Makkans decided that if they could not kill him they would impose a boycott on the Banu Hashim, the Prophet's ﷺ family. They were banished from the main town and could not trade or marry. They thought this would stop the spread of the new religion. The Prophet ﷺ and his family became very poor and often had little food. This lasted for four years until they were eventually allowed back into the city, but the Quraysh could not rest as the boycott did not have the desired effect. Finally, they decided to murder the Prophet ﷺ in his sleep, each of the clans taking part. In this way, they believed they could avoid a blood feud. The Prophet ﷺ was informed by Allah of their intentions and escaped Makkah that night with his best friend, Abu Bakr, to go to Medina.

After the Prophet Muhammad ﷺ and most of the Muslims migrated to Medina, the Makkans continued to plot about how to get rid of the Prophet ﷺ and the new religion. Occasional raids were carried out on the outskirts of the city. Throughout these difficulties, the Prophet ﷺ never tried to take revenge, but patiently endured, and continued to preach peacefully about the Oneness of Allah ﷻ.

Finally, the Quraysh planned to attack Medina. It was only then that Allah ordered the Prophet ﷺ to fight back in self-defense, to protect the people of Medina and the new religion of Islam. By taking part in actual battles, the Prophet Muhammad ﷺ was also able to show future Muslims the correct conduct in warfare.

In all, the Prophet Muhammad ﷺ fought in seven battles. In this book, we hear about four of them: The Battle of Badr, the Battle of Uhud, the Battle of the Trench and the Conquest of Makkah. They are narrated by a fictional character, Abdul Karim, a young man from Medina, who tells the stories from his point of view.

First, let's hear about what was happening in the city of Makkah just before the first battle.

Prologue

Makkah, March 624 (Sha'aban 2 AH)

Tensions were running high in Makkah. Humiliated and still furious at the escape of the Prophet Muhammad ﷺ from their failed assassination attempt two years ago, the Quraysh could not rest. They knew the Prophet ﷺ was in Medina, gaining in popularity by the day and that their very way of life, based on the worship of idols, was in peril. They took sacrifices to their idols to help, but to no effect. The empty stone faces stared out into the distance.

"O people of Makkah!" they cried. "We will raise an undefeatable army, and for it, we need every one of you to donate what you can of your valuables, your jewellery and your finery, which we will trade for the best armor and weapons Arabia has ever seen!"

The caravan of camels was loaded up with the finest goods that Makkah could muster before it set off for Syria. Even the women, who normally were not interested in trade or battles, donated many of their possessions.

Weeks later, as the caravan passed close to Medina on its return journey, a messenger ran up to Abu Sufyan, the leader of the Quraysh, and told him that the caravan was at risk of an imminent attack by Muslims. This alarmed the Quraysh who sprang into action, preparing themselves for battle as they set off towards Medina.

Being the most powerful tribe in Arabia, they had many strong warriors and plenty of weapons, armor, camels, and horses for battle. Although the Prophet Muhammad ﷺ and the Muslims had escaped persecution in Makkah, they were now in grave danger.

1
The Battle of Badr
13 March 624 CE (17 Ramadan, 2 A.H.)

Word was spreading around Medina that morning that the head of the Quraysh clan, Abu Sufyan, had a huge caravan loaded with riches and he would be passing nearby. I ran to find my friends. "Let's raid the caravan, we'll be rich!" I said.

"No way, Abdul Karim!" said my closest friend, Harith. "Don't you know it's Abu Sufyan's? He'll come and cut off your head!"

We all laughed.

"Let's see if we can spot it—I'll race you to the hill!" 'The hill' was our favourite lookout point on the edge of Medina.

"You won't be able to beat me!" said Shamsuddin who was the fastest runner.

We all sped away at top speed, and although I got a head start, Harith soon caught up with me, laughing as he passed. Shamsuddin also quickly passed me—how could I be so slow? We all arrived panting at the bottom of the hill. Shamsudin had a skin of water that he passed around as we caught our breath.

We climbed to the top of the hill where we could see for miles in the distance, hoping to get a glimpse of the richly laden caravan. I strained my eyes but could just see the rocky hills and desert landscape, flickering under the sun's heat. It must be passing a lot further than we thought.

We stayed there for a little while, standing up occasionally to look again and resting on the rocks until the sun was too hot.

"It's getting close to *dhuhr* prayer, I'm going back," I said. I never used to be interested in praying but when the Prophet ﷺ arrived two years ago, everything had changed; life was exciting.

Last year, I took my *shahada* with the Prophet ﷺ himself. It was an experience I shall never forget. I could hardly look at him, he was so majestic. My heart filled with so much love and I was in awe of his presence. He put me at ease though; he joked with me and ruffled my hair. I would do anything for him.

We made our way home through the market on the edge of Medina. On the town side of the market, there were stalls and rugs laid out on the dusty ground selling sweet-smelling incense, herbs and spices, juicy dates of all types, bread and other foods, clothing and linen, and heavy woven red and orange carpets. The sound of poetry and haggling filled the air.

We came to my favourite stall: the swordsmiths'. We admired one that was beautifully made, engraved with a Persian-looking design with a scabbard made of leather and blue silk. I would not have minded trying it out but had second thoughts as the stall owner appeared. He was a large, aged warrior with a huge beard and a dusty turban resting on his head. He was known for his short temper. Sometimes though, when he was in a good mood, he would tell us about the time he had fought in Makkah when the king and his elephants came to try to destroy the Kaaba. He said Allah had sent birds with small, burning hot stones to destroy the enemy and protect the Holy House.

But today he didn't look in a good mood, so I smiled pleasantly and asked how much some arrow tips were and then left. I took care to avoid the old lady who sat at the edge of the market with her heavily wrinkled face and no teeth. She would try to grab people's clothes and tell them their fortune. It says in the Qur'an that fortune-telling and divination is prohibited. The market used to be full of people hoping to tell you your destiny for half a dirham.

Beggars lined the edges of the market. I felt sorry for them but at least now there would be some food provided for them at the Prophet's ﷺ Mosque and by the Muslims, whenever they could. The Prophet ﷺ told us that there were so many heavenly blessings for feeding the poor.

Pungent smells of camel dung surrounded the outer part of the market. Camels, horses, sheep and goats were being bought and sold. Bedouins would arrive from the desert with their camels, their clothes dirty and unkept, trading and bargaining what they could.

I arrived at my house to wash and get ready to go to the Mosque.

"*As-salaamu 'alaikum,* Abdul Karim," Shukur greeted me as I pushed the fabric hanging aside that covered our front door and stepped into my house. It was a two-storey building that my father and my uncle made before I was born. It was made of mud and wood. Shakur was the father of the family from Makkah whom we agreed could stay with us. When everyone arrived from Makkah to escape the troubles there, the people of Medina offered to share their homes and their provisions. The Prophet ﷺ called us the *Ansar*—the Helpers—because of our generosity.

"*'Alaikum as-salaam,* Shakur," I said and sighed as I saw my bow and arrow had been moved again. His son, Shamil, aged ten, tended to use my belongings a little too much and without my permission. I also had to sleep in my parent's room so Shakur and his family could stay in my room. My mother hung a large piece of material between my bed and theirs to give us all some privacy.

Shakur was an African slave in Makkah. When he and his wife became Muslim, they endured much hardship. Abu Bakr, may Allah be well pleased with him, one of the Prophet's ﷺ closest Companions, had bought them for a high price and then gave them their freedom. They were so grateful.

I loved hearing his stories of when he was a boy in Africa over dinner. His melodious voice would tell us about his tribe and his family as well as scary tales of witch doctors and tribal lore.

I went upstairs to my room to change. Finding a fairly clean cloak to wear, I went outside and found the water to perform my *wu'du* that my mother always made sure was ready for us, and headed for the Mosque with Shakur and Shamil. My parents were already there. The Holy Prophet ﷺ had called a meeting.

Sa'd ibn Mu'adh, the leader of Medina, called out; "Everyone gather around! The Prophet ﷺ seeks the council of the *Ansar*!"

We gathered and sat in a large group.

Sa'd ibn Mu'adh stood up, and said, "O Prophet of Allah, is it us you wish to speak to?"

The Prophet ﷺ said, "Yes, it is you from whom I wish to hear, for I have travelled from my home and come to live with you."

He informed us that the Quraysh had summoned an army and were heading towards Medina to protect their caravan and that it was very likely they would attack the city. The Prophet ﷺ said we should meet them in battle, and that Angel Jibrail عليه وسلم, had promised us victory. But he, as a guest in our town, wanted to hear from the people of Medina, as he did not want us to get involved in something that was his conflict. Abu Bakr؇, Hamza؇ (the Prophet's ﷺ Uncle), `Umar؇, and `Ali؇ were all ready to defend the Prophet ﷺ —with their lives if need be.

I waited for the answer from the leader of our city.

Sa'd declared, "O Prophet of Allah, may our lives and souls and all our possessions be ransomed in your way!" In other words, the Prophet ﷺ had our complete support.

The Prophet ﷺ was happy with these words. He called Sa'd to him and kissed his face and said, "O Sa'd, may Allah reward you well."

It was decided—we were to prepare for battle. My heart was bursting with excitement to join the Prophet ﷺ in actual combat. I thought of the sword that my father gave me for my birthday last month and all the practice we did together. Then a flash of fear passed through my belly—the reality of war. I had never been in real combat before, and some of the Quraysh were formidable fighters.

I looked over at the Prophet ﷺ again, and my heart filled with peace and courage. Everything would be fine with the Prophet ﷺ on our side.

Waiting at home to leave, I still could not help

feeling a bit nervous as I packed my provisions. I decided my sword needed sharpening again so I went outside. I drew the blade over the stone, listening to the sound of steel and stone. I then practised many strokes, faster and faster, the midday sun flashing on the steel. All boys, and some of the girls, trained in sword fighting in Medina from an early age. We also trained in wrestling and shooting the bow. I wanted to be the best warrior in Medina one day. Feeling better, I sheathed my sword in its leather scabbard as I heard my father saying it was time to leave.

My mother waited in the doorway of our house with tears in her eyes but with a look of strength that her newly found faith gave her, filling my heart with even more courage.

My father smiled and hugged my mother and then said to us both: "We are serving a higher goal, for the Prophet's mission, indeed for Allah Himself. May He grant us victory!"

"*Ameen!*" we both replied.

We headed out towards Badr, about two days march from Medina, near where the caravan had passed. The Prophet ﷺ received news that the Quraysh armies were about one hour away and that they had slaughtered nine or ten beasts for food. That meant there were about one thousand men. I looked around and made an approximate count of our army. We only had about three hundred men, but included some of the best fighters in all of Arabia, such as `Ali ibn Talib؞, `Umar Ibn Khattab؞ and Hamza؞.

That night, camping out under the stars near my friends, Harith and Shamsuddin, I barely slept for all the excitement and nervous anticipation. The heavens seemed alive as I gazed into the vast blackness of night.

The next day, the Prophet ﷺ wisely positioned us with mountains to our sides and back to protect our army. He also stopped up the wells and built a water cistern so we would have water, but the enemy wouldn't.

We assumed our positions as the attacking army approached. There were flank after flank of the powerful clans of Makkah, their faces intent on destroying us. There were camels among their cavalry. I looked again at our small number and the reality dawned on me that they outnumbered us three to one. In my mind, I frantically tried to go over all the sword moves and throws that my father and uncle had shown me. I looked over at my friends who were looking serious and probably doing the same thing. Shamsuddin shifted uncomfortably from foot to foot.

Abu Jahl, whom I had heard was the worst of the enemy, called out, "If it is true what Muhammad says, then we are out to fight the God of the Heavens. But who that fights against me, is then fighting the God of the Heavens!"

"What's that idiot trying to say? That he is Allah?" I wondered aloud in surprise.

"As if!" Harith snorted.

Then a man from the tribe of Bani Makhzum said, "I swear to God that I will drink from the Muslims' cistern, or destroy it or die beside it!"

He ran towards our cistern well, but Hadrat Hamza tried to prevent him, cutting off his leg. I was shocked. Especially when the man dragged himself and his stump of a leg to the water cistern and threw himself in. Hamza immediately followed and killed him, the waters running with blood. Later, the enemy asked for water from the well, but it was said that everyone who drank from the well that day did not live to see the battle.

We were not to fight that day. Both armies retreated to their camps, planning to meet the next morning in battle. There was much silence as the men found places to camp for the night, each man preparing themselves for what looked like an unmatched battle.

During the evening, the Prophet ﷺ informed us of an *ayat* from the Qur'an:

"If victory you are seeking, victory has already come to you; and if you give over, it is better for you. But if you return, We shall return, and your host will avail you nothing though it be numerous; and that God is with the believers." (The Spoils:19)

Alhamdulillah, this greatly reassured us. That night, as we lay out under the stars, I thought again about the Holy verse.

In the morning, after praying for success, The Prophet ﷺ emerged from his small tent made of palm leaves and organized us into our ranks. I wanted to be right at the front, but new to battle, I was placed towards the rear. Of course, I went where the Prophet ﷺ ordered me to go, privately quite relieved.

As was the custom, the best warriors on both sides stepped forward to a duel. The enemy first sent out Utba bin Rabi'a, Shayba bin Rabi'a, and Walid, his son. They were big, fierce and armored, with more weapons than I thought possible. First, three of our Ansar clan rode out to meet them, but Abu Jahl said he wanted to fight his equals and had no quarrel with the people of Medina. So the Prophet ﷺ sent out `Ali ibn Abi Talib, Ubayda bin Harith, and Hamza ibn Abdul Muttalib to fight them.

In no time at all, Hadrat `Ali slew Walid; Hadrat Hamza slew Shayba; but Utba cut Hadrat Ubayda's leg off, spilling blood on the sand. `Ali and Hamza finished off Utba, and carried Ubayda to the Holy Prophet ﷺ. The Prophet ﷺ knelt down and said some words to him; we saw Ubayda smile as he died.

The battle began. I saw the Prophet ﷺ in the distance on the front line of the battle; he was bravely fighting off the enemy, one after the other, his close Companions around him. The Prophet ﷺ would push further and further into the midst of the battle, he looked as courageous as a lion, with no sign of fear, even though the Quraysh looked deranged and dark with fury. I prayed to Allah for support and mustered my courage and ran into the enemy, engaging one warrior and then another. An extra power I didn't know I had flowed through me. I felt invincible.

Then a youth my age challenged me. We were matched well, and his sword hit hard on my shield. As

I overpowered him, he came back with an ingenious move, wounding my side. I barely felt the injury and forged on until I struck him with a heavy blow. He retreated and limped away. I could not chase him as there were so many more behind him.

My fellow Muslims were being mortally wounded. Mihja received an arrow in his chest and the Prophet's Companion, Harith, an older man, also had his throat pierced by an arrow. Indeed, our numbers seemed few compared to the enemy and they seemed to be gaining much ground.

My next opponent was a large man with a face full of scars. He was experienced and strong and I had to use all my strength to fight him off. He hit my sword so hard that it flew out of my grip and landed a few yards away, so I immediately got him into a headlock and forced him to the ground and held him there, at the same time reaching for my sword.

I looked up and saw the Prophet praying to Allah and, to my amazement, scores of angels appeared, descending from the heavens, riding on horses with spears and swords in their hands!

The angels seemed to be made of light, yet powerful and frightening, heading towards the enemy.

STORIES FROM THE BATTLES OF THE PROPHET MUHAMMAD

Battle of Badr

Abu Sufyan's caravan *The Makkan army*

To Makkah

THE BATTLE OF BADR

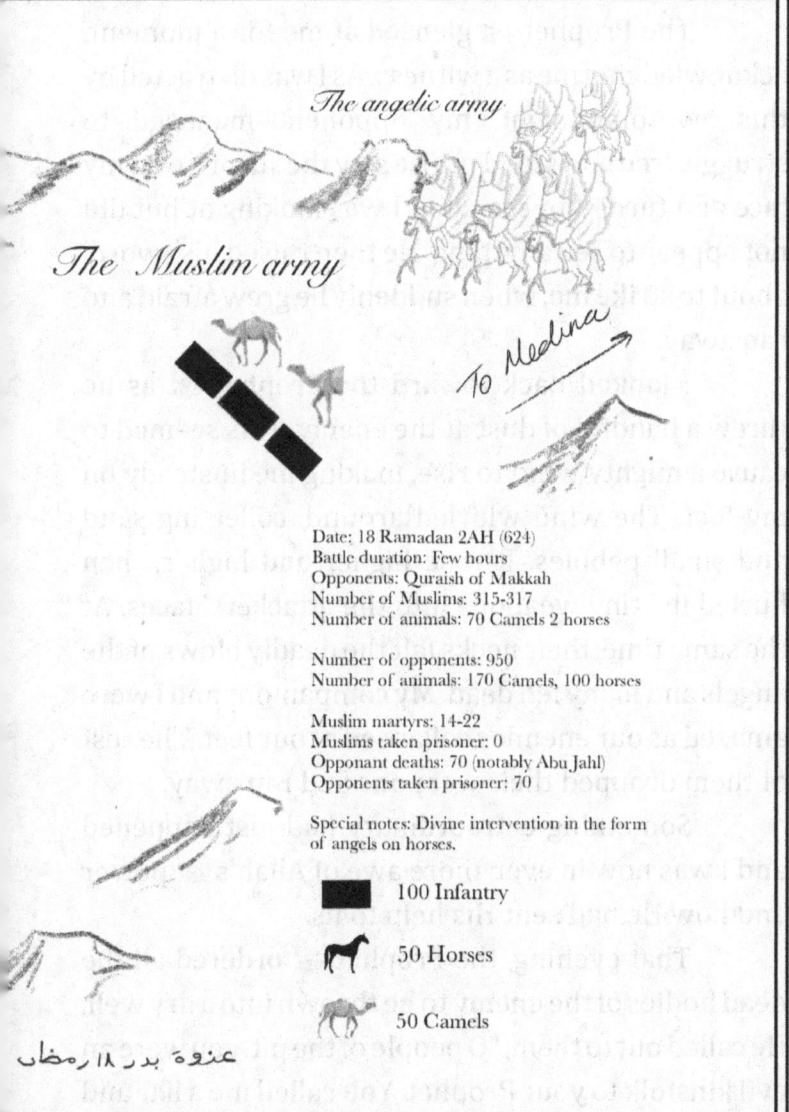

Date: 18 Ramadan 2AH (624)
Battle duration: Few hours
Opponents: Quraish of Makkah
Number of Muslims: 315-317
Number of animals: 70 Camels 2 horses

Number of opponents: 950
Number of animals: 170 Camels, 100 horses

Muslim martyrs: 14-22
Muslims taken prisoner: 0
Opponent deaths: 70 (notably Abu Jahl)
Opponents taken prisoner: 70

Special notes: Divine intervention in the form of angels on horses.

■ 100 Infantry

🐎 50 Horses

🐪 50 Camels

غزوة بدر ۱۸ رمضان

The Prophet ﷺ glanced at me for a moment, acknowledging me as a witness. As I was distracted by this awesome sight, my opponent managed to struggle free and stood up. He saw the surprise on my face and turned to see what I was looking at but did not appear to see anything. He then raised his sword, about to strike me, when suddenly he grew afraid and ran away.

I looked back toward the Prophet ﷺ as he threw a handful of dust at the enemy. This seemed to cause a mighty wind to rise, making me unsteady on my feet. The wind whirled around, collecting sand and small pebbles. It rose higher and higher, then hurled its' tiny weapons into the attackers' faces. At the same time, their necks felt the deadly blows of the angels and many fell dead. My companions and I were amazed as our enemies collapsed at our feet. The rest of them dropped their weapons and ran away.

Something extraordinary had just happened and I was now in even more awe of Allah's ﷻ power and how He had sent His help to us.

That evening, the Prophet ﷺ ordered all the dead bodies of the enemy to be thrown into a dry well. He called out to them, "O people of the pit, you were an evil kinsfolk to your Prophet. You called me a liar and expelled me from your city. Have you found what Allah has promised you is true? I have found that what my Lord promises me is true."

Some people asked him why he was calling to dead bodies, and the Prophet ﷺ said, "They hear as well as you do, but they cannot answer."

We set to work digging the graves of the Muslim Martyrs—those who had died for their religion. A messenger arrived who told us that the Prophet's beloved daughter, Ruqayyah؈, had died of an illness while we were away. This was indeed sad news. She was beloved to the Prophet ﷺ. I had not met her personally, but heard she was beautiful, kind and pious.

We were allowed some of the spoils from the battle. I was given a piece of armor; it was made of leather and metal and would come in very useful. The Prophet ﷺ told us that before this, the prophets were not allowed to have the spoils of war, but Allah had revealed a new verse of Qur'an that gave him permission.

We also had many prisoners. In normal Arab custom, prisoners were either killed or used as slaves. The Holy Prophet ﷺ announced that instead, we would keep them captive and offer ransoms for them.

He did not wish to harm them.

Over the next few weeks, we saw many people from Makkah come to claim their relatives and pay their ransom. We watched them arrive; some looked scared to enter Medina—they didn't know that we Muslims were not going to hurt them. I even heard that if they had no money, the Prophet ﷺ let them go anyway! This was new to all of us; we were not used to kindness in our old ways of warfare. The ransoms brought some much-needed money to our town.

At the *Jum'ah* prayer, the Prophet ﷺ told us about the revelations that he'd received in the battle. I especially remember these:

"When you were calling upon your Lord for help, and he answered you, 'I shall reinforce you with a thousand angels riding behind you.'" (The Spoils: 9)

"When thy Lord was revealing to the angels, I am with you; so confirm the believers. I shall cast into the unbelievers' hearts terror; so smite them above the necks, and smite every finger of them!" (The Spoils, 12)

Memories of the Battle of Badr will stay with me for the rest of my life. I will never forget them.

2
The Battle of Uhud

23 March 625 CE (7 Shawwal, 3 A.H.)

Things were stirring in our blessed town of Medina. A whole year had passed since the great Battle of Badr and we had heard that the Quraysh in Makkah were plotting their revenge.

Hubab ibn al-Mundhir ؓ and a group of scouts were sent out to find out information about the Makkans. We eagerly waited to hear what news they brought. In the meantime, the women, children and elderly were ordered to withdraw to safe quarters just in case of a sudden attack.

A cry came from the Prophet's ﷺ Mosque: "O leaders of Yathrib, leaders of the Sahaba, your Prophet is calling you to a war meeting. Come at once!"

My father hurried to join the meeting as he was one of the leaders. He returned within an hour and gathered our family around. He looked at me and said, "We must get you ready for battle, my son. The army of Quraysh are encamped by the mountain of Uhud—one day's journey from here. The Prophet ﷺ told us his dream about cattle and his sword."

My mother, who was always interested in dreams, asked, "Can you remember exactly what the dream was?"

My father thought for a moment. "Yes, the Prophet said: 'I saw in my dream a herd of cattle being slaughtered, and I saw a gash open upon the blade of my sword. Upon my back, I wore a suit of mail, and my hand I stuck into a collar of a suit of mail. The meaning of this dream is that the slaughtered cattle are my companions who will be martyred; the blade of my sword being broken means one of my family will be killed; and the metal coat of armor signifies Medina.'"

We all fell silent as we thought of the implications of this dream and its interpretation. The Prophet's ﷺ dreams were not like ours—they told of the future. It seemed that if we were to engage in battle again, there would be Martyrs and Medina would be protected, *insha'Allah*.

My father continued, "The Prophet said that his wish was to engage the enemy in a defensive position, only if the Quraysh actually attacked the city. However, there were many present at the meeting who wished to meet them in battle, including the Prophet's uncle, Hamza. After consideration, the Prophet said to us; 'Very well, so make ready for battle! If you are patient, you will again encounter help from Allah.'"

Excitement welled in my chest—another expedition accompanying the Holy Prophet ﷺ! I rushed to prepare myself, and my mother helped me. I could tell she was worried, as any mother would be. She forbade my father from going, as he had been unwell of late. He reluctantly agreed. I gathered my sword, sharpened my knife and checked my arrows. In my enthusiastic preparations, I did not think too much about what the Prophet ﷺ had said regarding patience.

Later at *Jumu`ah*, we sat and listened to the Prophet ﷺ. He told us what a noble deed it was, defending one's home and fighting for the sake of

Allah. The way he spoke filled me with such awe. The Prophet ﷺ and a few of his Companions then went to his rooms.

We were all in a state of readiness and excitement. My father and I had been practising the bow and arrow and I was actually quite a skilled shot. I had even shot a lizard, scampering along a rock, half a *ghalwa* away!

"Abdul Karim! Come, I have a gift for you." My father held out a leather quiver for the arrows we had made. He had made it himself in his workshop. He was a leatherworker by trade, making sandals mostly, but also some armor and quivers. I took the quiver and felt the smooth leather, probably camel hide, and admired his workmanship.

"I am sorry I cannot join you in battle, son."

I looked at him and looked away as a tear formed. I had been worried about him. I took a breath. "Don't worry father, I will be okay."

He put his hand on my shoulder. "I know— you are a strong fighter."

We heard the *adhan* and returned to the Mosque to join the `Asr prayer. After the prayer, some of the leaders of the Ansar were debating amongst themselves about the battle. The Prophet ﷺ came out from his apartment in full armor. He looked an impressive sight, full of nobility and *Allah's* Power.

Someone of the Ansar called out, "O *RasoolAllah*, if our opinion was contrary to your view, we beg your pardon, we will do whatever you say. If you think it is better not to leave the city, we will stay within and defend Medina when attacked."

However, the Prophet ﷺ said, "Nay, for when a prophet of Allah has girded himself for battle to combat the enemy of God, he will never lay down his arms, unless the Command of the Lord comes to him." The Prophet ﷺ then leapt upon his steed and sounded the battle-cry.

All of us grouped together and followed the Prophet ﷺ out of the city. Just as my companions and I were near the gates of Medina, we saw hundreds of men under `Abdullah bin Ubayd ibn Saul, turning on their heels, and heading back toward Medina. It looked like they were deserting us, fleeing from the battle and our army. How could anyone desert the Holy Prophet? It seemed to us like pure cowardice.

As we were walking along, I recounted stories of the great Battle of Badr to some of the younger boys: Usamah, `Abdullah and Thabit ibn Zaid, most of them not yet fourteen. They hoped if they walked with us and were not noticed, they would be allowed into the army as well, even though they were too young.

The Prophet ﷺ came up to us. I stood to attention and gazed at his Holy Countenance. He said, "We are facing a great battle and it is not the place for children. You will have to turn back from here and go home."

The boys' shoulders fell with disappointment to not be part of this important mission. I felt bad for them. But if the Prophet ﷺ said for them to go, it was for the best. The battlefield would be a dangerous place, they didn't know how brutal it could be.

Some of the older boys were to be selected though. Rafi' bin Hajid drew himself up on his toes to seem taller, as his best friend spoke up: "O *RasoolAllah*, please don't leave me out! I always throw Rafi when I am wrestling with him, so please let me be in your army too."

The Prophet ﷺ smiled at them. "Alright, show us. Wrestle with your friend and let us see."

They began, and I was impressed with their skills as wrestlers. Afterwards, we looked to the Prophet ﷺ who agreed that they could join us.

There were seven hundred of us in all, mostly men of all ages, with a few warrior women, as well as the women who brought food and medical supplies. I looked back briefly to see if I could see 'Asma, and saw her there in the group, she was chatting with the others. She glanced in my direction and I looked down, feeling a bit shy.

We marched on foot towards the mountain of Uhud across the dry, rocky desert. Our army only had two horses and a few camels. That night I was selected to patrol the outer fringes of our camp, and we climbed atop the hills to gaze out, searching for signs of the enemy. The stars were forming a blanket of light across the sky, as though expectantly watching for whatever may occur.

Later that night, I found a spot to rest, checking the space first for snakes and scorpions. I felt the enemy were like these poisonous creatures, heading towards us, intent on our defeat and hoping to extinguish the light of Islam. I was not going to let them do that, *insha'Allah*.

The next day, we positioned ourselves in front of the mountain of Uhud. This gave us a good vantage point: we were protected on all sides by the mountain with a small pass to the east. As we lined up, the Prophet ﷺ selected fifty of the best archers, and I was one of them. `Abdullah ibn Jubayri` was our commander. We were instructed to defend the pass against a likely attack from behind our lines.

The Prophet ﷺ said to our commander, "Whatever happens to us may happen, whether we lose or win. Unless you receive orders from me, do not under any circumstances leave your position. Even if all the unbelievers are slaughtered and nobody at all is left, if you have no word from me, do not leave your place."

We had our orders, so we waited on top of the hill—a good vantage point. We scanned the horizon...

There! The enemy approached.

As they came into clear view, we saw they were well-equipped: armed to the teeth with cavalry and camels. There were thousands of them. And wasn't that Khalid Ibn Walid travelling on one flank, sitting on a black horse? He was renowned for his strategy in battle, but we felt so invincible that I was sure not even he could harm us today, and there was Ikramah, Abu Jahl's son, on the other. Women called and chanted to the men from behind the army, shouting that they better kill the Muslims so that they could sleep in their beds.

The energy mounted. War drums boomed around the valley. Dust clouds billowed into the air from horse's hooves.

"*Allahu Akbar!*" the Prophet ﷺ shouted.

The rest of us began chanting as loud as we could, "*Allah, Allah, Allah!*"

The power that came from the Prophets' ﷺ cry and the *dhikr* of Allah ﷻ, made the drums seem like nothing. It cast fear into the hearts of the enemy, and made our hearts strong and ready.

The Prophet ﷺ said, "There is no escape from fate, fear cannot deter destiny; to fear the enemy of God is shameful, to confront him is honour and glory!"

Then the Prophet ﷺ drew his engraved sword in front of everyone and asked, "Who will take this sword and give it it's right?"

His Companion, Abu Dujanah؄, had the honour of taking this sword.

A renegade from the tribe of Aws stepped out and cried, "O, men of Ansar! I am sure you know me. I am Abu Amir." He waited. He seemed to think some of the Ansar would desert our ranks and join him.

Someone from the Ansar replied, "Oh yes, we know you very well for the impious, corrupt person that you are, but make sure you know this well: the Lord will not fulfil your desires."

The Quraysh then demanded single combat.

They sent Talha out, a renowned warrior. The Prophet ﷺ sent `Ali to fight him. He finished Talha in a few strokes of his sword.

Talha's son, enraged at seeing his father lying in the dust, came out next, and the Prophet ﷺ sent Hamza. Again, we were victorious.

Angered, the Quraysh charged forth and the battle began in earnest. We fired our arrows when we had the chance, but we had to ensure there were enough for a possible attack from the rear. We could only look on from our vantage point, frustrated at not being able to join in the fighting, but we had our orders.

The standard of the Makkans passed from man to man as each one was destroyed by our most fierce fighters. Sa'ad bin Abu Waqqas shot an arrow straight at Abu Talha from the Makkans; the standard continued to be passed between no less than seven men in the space of a short time. The smell of sweat and blood filled our nostrils. Their women continued to drum in the background.

`Ali ibn Abi Talib fought with such might that it seemed every man of the enemy must have felt his sword. Men seem to fall to the ground with one blow, such was his strength. No wonder the Prophet ﷺ named both him and Hamza, the Lions of Allah. They ploughed through the enemy with an unstoppable power.

Finally, the army of the Quraysh retreated. As the Muslims pushed forward, the women at the back of the Makkan army broke ranks and fled. The rest of the men soon followed, leaving all their provisions and possessions on the battleground. Believing they had won, my Muslim brothers lowered their arms and began to collect the booty.

Our commander, `Abdullah ibn Uways said, "There is now no need to guard this pass. Ahead of us is all clear—let us go out into the battlefield."

If we didn't go and claim some of the booty, the others would have all of it. We looked at `Abdullah ibn Jabayr for instruction.

He said, "The Messenger of Allah told us not to leave this place under any circumstances, unless he gave the command!"

It was true the Prophet ﷺ had said that, but our commander had told us to go to the battlefield and we wanted our share of the reward. *It will be fine*, I thought, as I joined the others. Only a few remained on the hill, including my friend, Harith. He shook his head as he looked at me leaving. *I'll get something for him*, I thought to myself. *He'll be glad I went.*

We ran down to the battlefield and started filling our bags with what we could find. Suddenly, shouts echoed over the desert from behind us. I looked up and was horrified to see that our position was being overwhelmed by Khalid ibn Walid and the enemy, having made a surprise rear attack. The helmet I had been stuffing into my bag suddenly felt like ice as I realised what we had done.

The cold feeling of fear stayed with me as I got up and ran towards them. It was too late to help the archers—they had all been killed. I saw Harith lying there, a stab of pain and anguish shot through my heart.

The enemy had now taken full control of an attack at the rear. Enraged, I ran at them, using my sword to attack one soldier and then another, the anger pushing my shame away.

I stumbled and fell, and saw Hamza close by, lying on the ground and clutching a spear that had pierced his heart. No! My heart sank as I tried to move towards him, but the enemy stopped me in my tracks. About to receive a fatal blow, I used my shield and warded off the strikes, then began my own attack. I glanced over at Hamza again and I felt nauseous. A slave was cutting out his liver and his ears.

"The Prophet has been killed!" someone shouted from the fray.

My body froze; the fight drained out of me. `Umar ؓ stood in the distance with a stunned look on his face. The enemy was gaining power. I had to move, to change position. I ran to the back of the fighting and came upon a group of twelve men fighting valiantly, and in the middle was the Prophet ﷺ. Relief flooded my chest.

I fought off the enemy again as best I could, but many had not seen him. "He's alive! The Prophet has not been killed!" I shouted, but the battle's intensity stole my words. A big oaf kept pushing me in the chest, so I couldn't catch my breath.

Ka'b bin Malik ؓ cried out, "O Muslims, here is the Prophet. He is here!"

Unfortunately, the enemy also heard these cries and focused on where he stood. The Muslims were now forming a shield so the Prophet ﷺ would not be hurt. Men were falling, martyred.

Umm Ummara ؓ, one of our fiercest warrior women, positioned herself between the enemy and the Holy Prophet ﷺ to protect him. She was incredible, fighting off one warrior after the next. But the enemy was so intent, they closed in on him. One of them hit our Holy Prophet ﷺ, and blood poured from his face. Those cursed men were laid to the ground by our fighters. Bits of metal had lodged into the face of the Prophet ﷺ and Abu Ubaydah bent over him to remove them with his teeth, damaging his own teeth. The Prophet's ﷺ daughter, Fatima, came rushing to the battlefield and tried to help her father as the intense battle continued. The Muslims were forced back.

The Companions, on seeing the Prophet ﷺ so badly injured, said, "If only you would invoke a curse against them."

He replied, "I was not sent to curse, but I was sent as a summoner and as a mercy. O Allah, guide my people for they do not know."

Then Umar said, "My mother and father be your ransom, O Messenger of Allah! The prophet Noah invoked a curse against his people when he said, '*My Lord, do not leave one of the rejectors upon the Earth*.' (71:26) Had you invoked a curse like that against us, we would have been destroyed to the last man. Your back has been trodden on, your face has been bloodied and your tooth has been broken, and yet you refuse to utter anything but good. You have said, 'O Allah, forgive my people for they do not know.'"

Then, Wahab bin Kabu؂ arrived on the battlefield, a noble-looking man. He engaged the enemy in an impressive onslaught, fighting twenty attackers at a time. This pushed the enemy back. Wahab ر fell though; another Martyr heading straight for the Divine Presence.

Even though the enemy almost claimed the better of us, we managed one final push and there was a lull in the fighting. The Prophet ﷺ decided to withdraw. We moved to a more protected part of the mountain and I sat exhausted on a rock. A wound on my arm throbbed. The sun beat down. I chose a place away from the others, not wanting to be seen.

We expected the enemy to scale the mountain, but for some reason they could not manage it. My friend told me it was because the Prophet ﷺ had prayed to Allah for extra support.

Abu Sufyan shouted out from the bottom of the mountain, "Is Muhammad with you?"

The Prophet ﷺ indicated that no one should reply. Abu Sufyan then asked about Abu Bakr؂ and `Ali ؂ and `Umar؂ ...but no one answered.

Abu Sufyan said, "This means to say that they are dead; the backbone of Islam is broken. We have attained our goal; this new religion is extinguished."

STORIES FROM THE BATTLES OF THE PROPHET MUHAMMAD

Battle of Uhud

Date: 7 Shawwal, 2 AH (625)
Battle duration: 4+ hours
Opponents: Quraysh of Makkah

Number of Muslims: 700
Number of animals: 70 Camels
2 horses

Number of opponents: 3000
Number of animals: 1000 Camels, 200 horses

Muslim martyrs: 62-75
Muslims taken prisoner: 0
Opponent deaths: 22-35
Opponents taken prisoner: 0

 100 Infantry

 50 Cavalry

 100 Camels

THE BATTLE OF UHUD

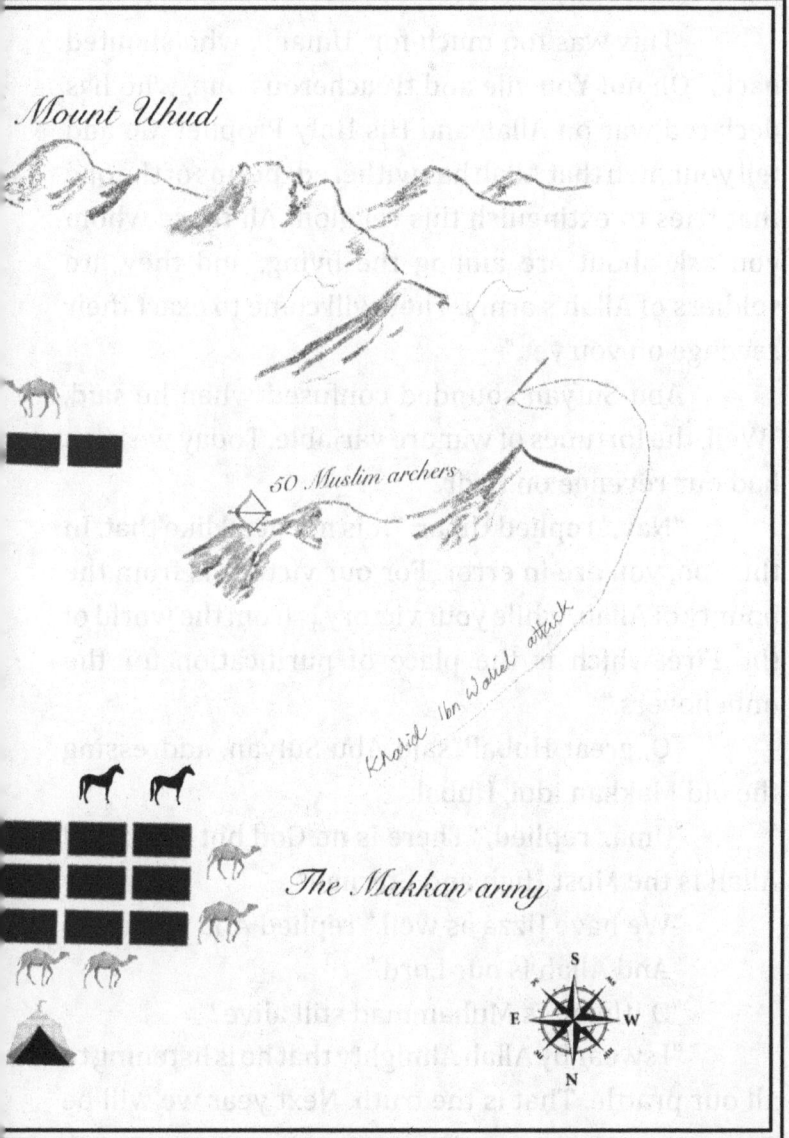

This was too much for `Umar, who shouted back, "Oh no! You vile and treacherous one, who has declared war on Allah and His Holy Prophet. Go and tell your men that Allah has withered the lips of the one that tries to extinguish this religion! All those whom you ask about are among the living, and they are soldiers of Allah's army. They will come to exact their revenge on you yet."

Abu Sufyan sounded confused when he said, "Well, the fortunes of war are variable. Today we have had our revenge on Badr."

"Nay," replied Umar. "It is not at all like that. In this too, you are in error. For our victory is from the bounty of Allah, while your victory is from the world of the Fire which is the place of purification for the unbelievers."

"O, great Hubal!" said Abu Sufyan, addressing the old Makkan idol, Hubal.

`Umar replied, "There is no God but Allah and Allah is the Most High and Eternal!"

"We have Uzza as well," replied Abu Sufyan.

"And Allah is our Lord."

"O `Umar, is Muhammad still alive?"

"I swear by Allah Almighty that he is listening to all our prattle. That is the truth. Next year we will be back to measure ourselves against you, then you will see how it shall be." (1)

With that, Abu Sufyan left. It seemed the Quraysh had decided to ride back to Makkah.

We followed the Prophet ﷺ back to the battlefield and helped to dig the graves of those who had fallen and the women tended to the wounded. The Prophet ﷺ wandered the field, stopping at each of the dead, gazing down for a while and making prayers. He stopped and prayed for Harith. I knew he was now in a better place. We saw the tears of the Prophet ﷺ fall on those blessed Martyrs. When he came to his beloved uncle, Hamza, he bent down to embrace him. His deep sadness was clear to see.

Later, as we prayed together for the dead, the Holy Prophet ﷺ was overcome many times as we all were. Great sadness lay in our hearts, but we knew the Martyrs had died a most honourable death serving Allah Almighty. They had reached Paradise.

The Holy Prophet ﷺ spoke; "I bear witness that these friends of mine placed their own self-interest last, and that they surrendered their lives and

---

1.*Extract from Hajja Amina's book: Muhammad, the Messenger of Islam* souls in Allah's cause. Yes, in the eternal world to come, on that second Day of Gathering, those who were wounded for the sake of Allah will rise from their graves, blood flowing afresh from their wounds. No man nor angel will at that instance not feel passionate love for the colour of that Martyr's blood, and indeed, will become intoxicated on the scent issuing from it."

An *Ayat* from the Qur'an was revealed about what happens to those who die in Allah's way, which gave comfort to us:

"'And never think of those who have been killed in the cause of Allah as dead. Rather, they are alive with their Lord, receiving provision, rejoicing in what Allah has bestowed upon them of His bounty, and they receive good tidings about those [to be martyred] after them who have not yet joined them—that there will be no fear concerning them, nor will they grieve. They receive good tidings of favor from Allah and bounty and [of the fact] that Allah does not allow the reward of believers to be lost—those [believers] who responded to Allah and the Messenger after injury had struck them. For those who did good among them and feared Allah is a great reward. Those to whom hypocrites said, "Indeed, the people have gathered against you, so fear them." But it [merely] increased them

in faith, and they said, "Sufficient for us is Allah, and [He is] the best Disposer of affairs." (Family of Imran; 169-173)

As I stood before the newly filled graves, I could not help but think of the Prophet's ﷺ sadness and the great number who had died. Shame and humiliation flowed through me. We had deserted our Companions on the hill in favour of greed. Harith and Hamza and many other excellent Muslims died because of our bad choice. The Prophet ﷺ had been wounded and in danger of his life. I could not face my friends, my family, and especially the Prophet ﷺ. I felt like the worst traitor, only fit for the rubbish dump, wishing that I had died instead of those noble ones.

My comrades, who had also deserted the hill, wore the same expressions of shame. Some of them, braver than I, approached the Prophet ﷺ to express their deep remorse.

The Prophet ﷺ called everyone together. "Be not overly distraught, for you have been forgiven. The conquest of Makkah is near."

Great relief flooded through me. The Prophet ﷺ said we were forgiven, *alhamdulillah*. I was also relieved to not get a severe punishment for disobeying orders. My heart filled with even more love for our Prophet ﷺ, in whom I could find no fault.

Some *ayats* of Qur'an were revealed to us about our weakness in the battle:

"And Allah had certainly fulfilled His promise to you when you were killing the enemy by His permission until [the time] when you lost courage and fell to disputing about the order [given by the Prophet] and disobeyed after He had shown you that which you love. Among you are some who desire this world, and among you are some who desire the Hereafter. Then he turned you back from them [defeated] that He might test you. And He has already forgiven you, and Allah is the possessor of bounty for the believers." (Family of Imran:152)

"Indeed, those of you who turned back on the day the two armies met, it was Satan who caused them to falter on account of their weakness [for material gains]. But Allah forgave them. Indeed, Allah is Oft-Forgiving and Most Forbearing." (Family of Imran: 155)

We headed back to Medina carrying the wounded, of which there were many. Excruciating pain throbbed in my arm from a deep wound. I was glad to walk in through the front door of my home and fall into my mother's arms. Exhaustion overcame me. I retreated to my bed and she tended my wounds. I didn't feel like talking much.

Shortly after, my father told me that the Prophet ﷺ had set out once again with seventy strong men; joined by another six hundred, and those only lightly wounded. The intention was to pursue the enemy who were bound to return, having almost achieved their goal of wiping us out. However, the Prophet ﷺ returned to Medina soon after he left; it seemed that the enemy chose not to return after all.

Most households that night cried, in grief of those we had lost. I thought sadly of Harith, remembering all the times we'd had. And Hamza, one of the most noble of men, a great warrior and one of the Prophet's ﷺ noble family.

In the morning we heard that the Prophet ﷺ prayed for the enemy who had injured him by the sword. The Prophet ﷺ did not order retaliation for the person who did that to him. Instead, the Prophet ﷺ said, "O Allah, forgive my people for they do not know."

The Prophet ﷺ was so forgiving, and he'd said Allah had forgiven us—the ones who deserted our posts—so why was I still so remorseful?

Then, I remembered the *ayat* from Qur'an:

"And if, when they wronged themselves, they had come to you, [O Muhammad], and asked forgiveness of Allah and the Messenger had asked forgiveness for them, they would have found Allah accepting of repentance and Merciful. (The Women:64)

I had to go and see the Prophet ﷺ himself. During a quiet moment, when the Prophet ﷺ was sitting on his own, I forced myself to approach him. Feeling like the worst person to ever walk the Earth, I kept my eyes downcast. I could barely look at his face. As he turned, I caught his eye for a split second and he looked at me with such compassion, such love, my eyes filled with tears. I knew then that he had truly forgiven me, and that now I could forgive myself.

"I am sorry, my Prophet."

He smiled, and his words reminded me that we have yet to attain perfection. I remembered what the Prophet ﷺ had told us before battle; "If you are patient, you will again encounter help from Allah."

I saw that day, what it meant to be patient. Even if all the world was crying out to do something, and logic said otherwise, I would never doubt the words of the Prophet ﷺ. That meant having strength on another level, more difficult to come by than fighting a hundred brave warriors on the battlefield.

3
The Battle of the Trench

23 December 626 CE (Dhul Qada, 5 A.H.)

We had heard, through the Prophet's ﷺ scouts, that a huge force was being gathered to fight against us. The tribes of the Bani Nadir and the Bani Qaynuqa, who had been expelled from Medina because of their assassination attempt on the Messenger of Allah ﷺ last year, had been meeting with the Quraysh. They had also united with the Ghatafan tribe, the Bani Murra, Bani Asad, the Bani Sulaym, and the tribes of Ashja. It seemed as if the whole of Arabia was pitched against us.

How could they not hear the message of the Prophet ﷺ? He only brought peace, hope, and mercy. Could they not see that?

Over the last year, the Quraysh had been persecuting us by sending small bands of warriors to attack those who left Medina and I was starting to think it wasn't safe to leave the city. Forty of my father's friends were invited to teach Islam to some of the nearby tribes, and they were all assassinated on the way. I couldn't believe it—all of those men had memorized the Qur'an, they were the guardians of Allah's Words.

My father attended the war meeting with the other elders of the *Ansar*. I wanted to, but I was still too young so I waited outside. Sometime later, the men began to leave. I moved towards them to find out what was happening.

Salman al Farsi appeared at the door. He was different to a lot of us; his pale skin and fine features showed that he was from the north. I had heard he was once a Christian and then a slave. He smiled at me but with a look of concern. "Make haste. We haven't got much time," he said.

I waited until my father appeared and eagerly

questioned him. "Father, are we going into battle again?"

"This time is a bit different, my son. Salman has suggested a good plan to the Messenger of Allah who accepted it. We are going to dig a trench across the north-west border of Medina to stop the attack. These are methods used by the great armies of Persia which we hope will grant us success, *insha'Allah*. The Quraysh and whoever has sided with them could be here in a matter of days, so we must work hard to complete the trench."

A few thousand men and boys were gathered to dig the trench and we were divided into groups of ten. I was so pleased to be placed fairly near the Prophet ﷺ. Each team had to dig a ditch seventy feet long, thirty feet wide and fifteen feet deep around the borders of Medina. The completed trench would be about three miles long.

The ground was hard, rocky, and dry, and it was exhausting work. I paused for a moment, leaning on my shovel, with sweat streaming down my face. I looked over at the Prophet ﷺ. He seemed calm and unruffled and to be working faster than everyone else. He seemed to have the strength of one hundred men, even though he was three times my age.

We kept digging night and day, only resting when we needed to and barely stopping to eat. Sometimes food was passed around, but there was so little food in Medina and we went for whole days without it. We would sing some verses to keep us going:

"We're the ones who've pledged ourselves to Muhammad; we pledged to do jihad for as long as we live."

"The enemy is attacking us to make us leave the truth, but we stubbornly refuse to oblige."

The Prophet ﷺ replied to our verses, saying:

"O Lord! Had You not guided us in Your Grace and Mercy, how sorry would have been our state! We would have not known about worship, nor would we have followed the path of guidance!"

A huge boulder was stopping progress. None of our tools or the strongest men could budge it. The Prophet ﷺ was notified and he came over with his pickaxe. He cried, "*Bismillah ir-Rahman ir-Rahim!*" and struck the rock.

He struck it three times, and each time, a

section of the rock broke away. "*Allahu Akbar!*" The Prophet ﷺ exclaimed. "By Allah, at this moment I behold the red roofs of Damascus! Now I see the gates to the city of Sanaa." After another strike, he said, "By Allah, I now behold the white houses of Mada'in belonging to the Khosroes. The arm rings of Khosroes will be slipped onto Saraqa's wrist."

I was told that the Prophet ﷺ was predicting that Islam would spread to all of these lands. I looked around at our men listening to the Prophet ﷺ, and those working hard in the distance. We were probably gravely outnumbered by the Quraysh, yet the Prophet ﷺ predicted success in the future. It was all in Allah's Hands.

We were making good progress as the days wore on, even though the sun seemed hotter by the day and I could feel my strength dwindling. '*Bismillah ir-Rahman ir-Rahim*!' I would say to myself to keep going, and it always gave me the extra strength I needed.

Amazingly, we finished within twenty days, with Allah's Support. The trench was huge, stretching out in either direction, forming a protective barrier. How were we going to get out afterwards? Our city was now cut off from the rest of the world.

It turned out that we had finished it just in time. The very next day we heard from the scouts that a huge army was approaching. They estimated ten thousand men. The women and children were sent to the far corners of the city for safety while we prepared for a defensive battle. Again, we were outnumbered by over three men to one.

The first few enemy riders cantered up on their horses. Because we did not meet them for battle, they confidently rode up towards the gates of Medina as if to claim victory—that is, until they spotted the huge trench. Confusion appeared on their faces as they looked beyond the trench and saw our archers' arrows trained on them. They swiftly turned around to rejoin their men and we watched them gallop away. They had no choice but to set up camp, and probably had little preparations for one. *Insha'Allah*, we hoped they would not last long.

We were well-defended behind the large mounds of earth, with plenty of rocks on hand in case they tried to cross the trench. We also had our archers, including myself, at the ready.

Meanwhile, there were whispers among our ranks that the Bani Qurayza - a Jewish tribe who lived in Medina and who had signed a peace contract with the Prophet - had secretly sided with the enemy. This was unnerving as their fort was located behind us, inside Medina, near to where the women and children were. We could not leave our post long enough to go and interrogate the Bani Qurayza. We just had to hope it was not true. Some of our men went to check on them and everyone seemed safe, at least for the time being.

We waited all night, lined up along the trench, taking turns to rest while others kept watch. We had to be vigilant—there were several miles of the trench to watch and we couldn't take our eyes off it for a moment.

At first light, we heard shouts as the enemy attacked; arrows rained down on us and we fired back in return. They began to try and cross the trench with no success. The enemy's huge number was threatening - we would be easy targets if they managed to get across.

Salman's trench seemed to be working: none of the enemy soldiers succeeded in crossing. They could have stretched themselves out across the whole line of our trench and attacked all at once, but they knew this was too great a risk because we Muslims had superior hand-to-hand battle skills and they

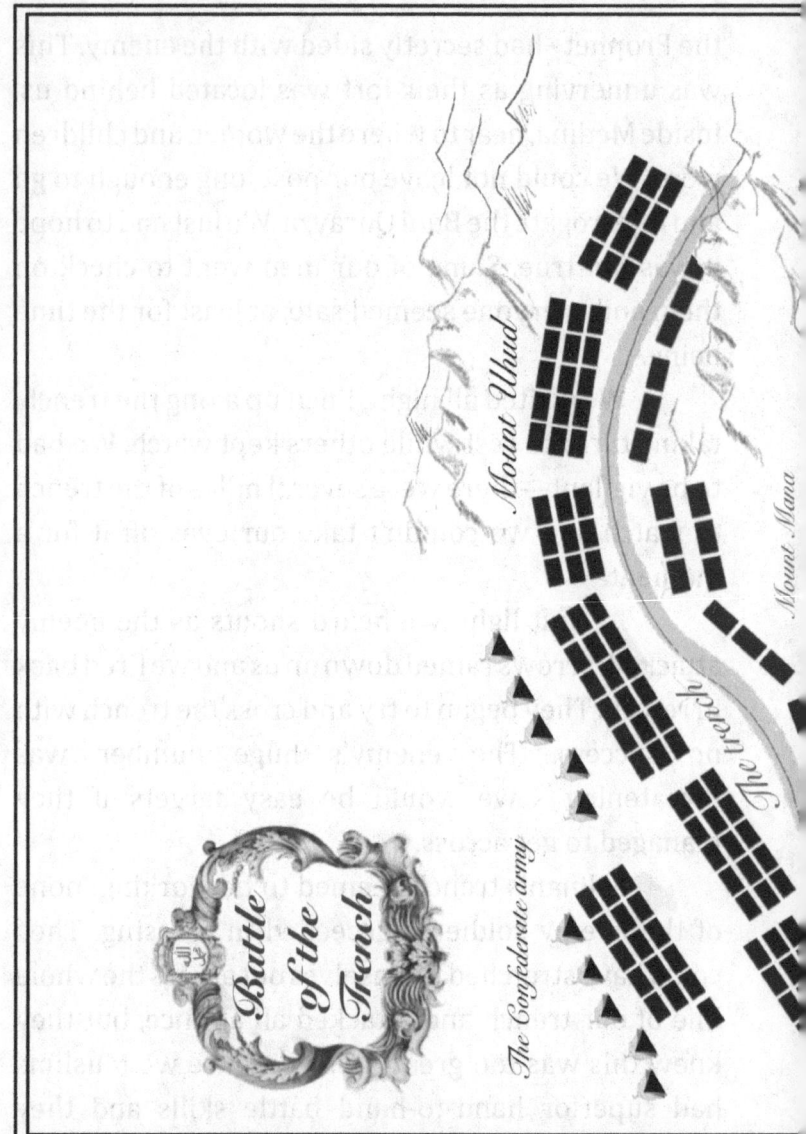

THE BATTLE OF THE TRENCH

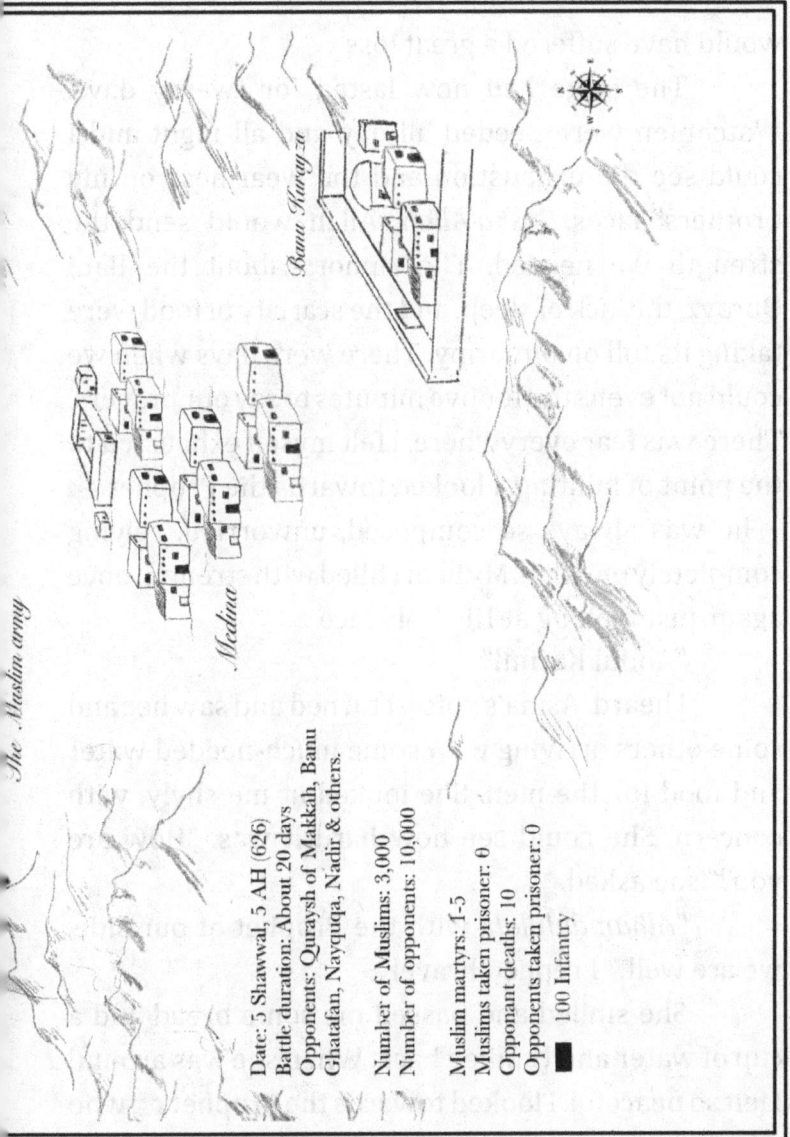

The Muslim army

Date: 5 Shawwal, 5 AH (626)
Battle duration: About 20 days
Opponents: Quraysh of Makkah, Banu Ghatafan, Nayquqa, Nadir & others.

Number of Muslims: 3,000
Number of opponents: 10,000

Muslim martyrs: 1-5
Muslims taken prisoner: 0
Opponent deaths: 10
Opponents taken prisoner: 0

■ 100 Infantry

would have suffered a great loss.

The siege had now lasted for twenty days. Watchmen were needed all day and all night and I could see the exhaustion and the weariness on my brothers' faces. *Insha'Allah*, Allah would send the strength we needed. The rumors about the Bani Qurayz, the lack of sleep, and the scarcity of food were taking its toll on our army. There were days when we could not even stop for five minutes to say our prayers. There was fear everywhere. I felt myself exhausted to the point of fainting. I looked towards the Prophet ﷺ —he was always so composed, unworried, relying completely on Allah. My heart filled with strength once again, just looking at His Holy face.

"Abdul Karim!"

I heard 'Asma's voice. I turned and saw her and some others arriving with some much-needed water and food for the men. She looked at me shyly, with concern. She could see how hard it was. "How are you?" she asked.

"*Alhamdulillah*, with the Prophet at our side, we are well," I replied bravely.

She smiled and passed me some bread and a cup of water and I smiled back. When she was around I felt so peaceful. I looked towards the Prophet ﷺ who saw us and also smiled. *InshaAllah*, one day, when this was all over, I planned to ask to her to marry me.

The Prophet ﷺ would position himself in the most dangerous areas, and he was concerned about us—the Ansar, and our beloved city—being under attack for embracing this new religion. But our leaders reassured the Prophet ﷺ that what he had brought us was worth more than all the diamonds in the world.

Day after day, the siege continued until at last —frustrated at their lack of success—the enemy decided to send their fiercest warriors on horseback across the trench. First, was the famous 'Amr ibn 'Abdu Wudd, an old but fearless warrior. It was said he had vowed not to wash or comb his hair until Badr was avenged. I was glad I didn't have to share a tent with him! Behind him came Umar Ibn Khattab's ر brother, Dirar, then Hubayra bin Abi Wahb, and Ikrama ibn Abu Jahl.

'Amr ibn 'Abdu Wudd shouted out, "Where are you who started this business of *La ilaha il Allah*? Who wishes to destroy all inherited tradition by this claim of One God only, and resurrection after death? I have come and I am ready! I challenge you to send me a man who will fight me. Send out one of your fighters!"

The noble Companions were unsure who they would send out.

'Ali stepped forward. "I will go!" he said.

The Prophet was initially reluctant to agree. But insults were being thrown at the Prophet and 'Ali could stand it no more. He stood up and said, "At least let me prove I am his equal!"

The Prophet then placed his own armor on 'Ali and gave him his sword, *Dhul Fiqar*. I would have gone myself, of course, but Ali was a stronger fighter than I was. If I were to fail, the enemy would have felt encouraged. The Prophet prayed for 'Ali, then kissed him on his head.

As 'Ali moved forward on foot, 'Amr approached him on horseback. We all wondered at the obvious inequality between the two. 'Amr liked to give his opponents three wishes so he demanded these from 'Ali.

'Ali replied: "That you may come to reason and accept Islam!"

"What?!" roared 'Amr. "You still persist in asking me this?"

"What else do have I to persist in?" 'Ali replied.

'Amr jumped down from his horse and cut the

animal with his sword, to the shock of those watching. Then he rushed at 'Ali ؑ with his sword raised and struck out, cleaving 'Ali's shield in two. 'Ali ؑ drew *Dhul Fiqar* from its sheath and, crying, "*Allahu Akbar!*" he struck 'Amr with such a blow that he fell down dead.

We all cheered; one of their best fighters was down.

Munabbih stepped out from the enemy lines and was met by Zubayr, who killed him, again with one stroke. Then others from the enemy's side came out: Umar's ؓ brother and Abu Jahl's son: Ikrama and Khubayr Abu Wahab. When 'Ali ؑ and Zubayr ؓ met them to fight, the enemy's best warriors then turned and fled back to their camp. 'Ali ؑ and Zubayr ؓ could have gone after them, but these were against Ali's principles: he never pursued a fleeing enemy. Angry at the humiliating loss of some of their greatest fighters, the enemy barraged us with a new rain of arrows.

The next day we heard that the Bani Qurayza Jews had indeed betrayed us. They decided to attack near the women's quarters, but Safiya bint Abu Muttalib ؓ and the other women fought off the traitors, hitting them with tent poles. They retreated back into their fort.

The Prophet ﷺ prayed to Allah: "O my Lord, do not test this band of Muslims who assert Your Oneness with overly hard trials! They will never turn away from You, so don't expose their faces to the enemy's arrows for much longer!"

The Prophet ﷺ continued to pray: "O Lord! Please send Your Divine Support to this small band of Muslims who believe in Your Unity. If it is Your Will, send against their foes an angelic army, or turn the elements of nature that obey Your Command against the enemy. Fulfill Your promise to me, however You choose to do that!" He then turned to us and said, "The enemy may do whatever he likes, the Lord Almighty is on our side!"

Just as he spoke, a wind started to blow; initially, it was light but it soon became so fierce that we had to kneel and keep low to the ground. I saw the enemy across the trench, backing away with their arms up to protect their faces from the wind and the sand. As the wind grew more powerful, they stumbled and fell. I could just make out their outline through the sand-filled air, crawling towards their camp and their horses. Eventually, it became impossible to see anything at all.

As the wind subsided and the sand settled, we looked across the trench - the enemy was nowhere to be seen.

Hudhayfa bin Yamam ؓ was sent to check the situation. When he returned, he said he'd spoken to six unknown men on horseback who said, "O Hudhayfa, go and tell your friend that Allah has turned against his enemies to destroy them." The Prophet ﷺ smiled very broadly and told us that they were, in fact, angels sent by Allah.

Allahu Akbar! Allah had saved us from an army ten times our size. We assessed our casualties which were only five. One of the five was the noble companion Sa'd ibn Mu'adh ؓ who had received serious wounds and was moved to a special tent in the Prophet's Mosque where the Prophet ﷺ himself tended to him.

He heard about how Nuaym ؓ, an important man from the tribe of Ashja', helped to weaken the resolve of the enemy. Nuaym ؓ had secretly become Muslim and thought about how to use his position amongst the enemy to help win the war for us. Nuaym ؓ first went to the Bani Qurayza, who had just betrayed us, and told them the Quraysh and Ghatafan tribes were about to give up and leave them to the hands of the Muslims. Nuaym suggested that, for security, they should demand that some of the Quraysh and Ghatafan should join their side as reinforcements and proof of their commitment to battle. The Bani Qurayza agreed this was the best course of action as they could see the siege was wearing thin for the Confederate enemy, whose supplies and morale were very low.

Nuaym then went to Abu Sufyan and told them he had just had a meeting with the Bani Qurayza, who had reunited with the Prophet ﷺ and made a secret treaty with him. To convince the Prophet ﷺ of their loyalty, he said they had promised to give him some hostages from the Quraysh and Ghatafan tribes.

Abu Sufyan was alarmed at this news and immediately sent a message to the Bani Qurayza suggesting that they must join them in battle the next day as their supplies were running low and they needed to strike as soon as possible. The Bani Qurayza agreed, but only if Abu Sufyan sent seventy of his men as hostages.

Of course, Abu Sufyan now thought that what Nuaym said was true and refused to send the hostages. He told the Bani Qurayza they no longer had the support of the Quraysh—let the Muslims deal with them. The relations between them completely broke

THE BATTLE OF THE TRENCH

down and the Bani Qurayza left the battleground and retreated to their fort.

I am sure that they bitterly regretted that they had broken their treaty with us, having lost the alliance with the Quraysh. The treaty between the Jews of Medina and the Muslims had been there to ensure mutual cooperation between us. Their treachery might have cost us the battle. I wondered what the Prophet ﷺ would command us to do... The crime of breaking a treaty by treachery was very serious.

The Prophet ﷺ received a command from Allah to go and deal with the Bani Qurayza straightaway. We marched over to their quarters, without even changing our battle dress.

On the way, the Prophet ﷺ said, "Should the Bani Qurayza show any sign of regret then I will pray for Allah to forgive them."

I knew the Prophet ﷺ would show great leniency, as he always had in the past. Hopefully, they would show regret and ask for forgiveness.

We watched 'Ali go up to the gates of the fort and the Bani Qurayza shouting things at him. 'Ali returned, an angry look upon his face and told us they only said terrible things about the Prophet ﷺ. It was decided that we would lay siege to their fort.

The siege lasted for twenty days. Finally, a Bani Qurayza representative came out and declared that they would accept the judgment of Sa'd ibn Mu'adh as there was a long-term pact between his tribe and the Bani Qurayza. He had been badly injured but gave the verdict that the men-at-arms should be killed and the women and children be given as captives and their belongings confiscated. This followed the laws of the Torah.

If only they had sought pardon from the Prophet ﷺ himself, a much lighter sentence would have been passed. The Prophet ﷺ always forgave. That was a very hard day for all of us. This ayat from the Qur'an was revealed about this tragic event:

"Behold! They came on you from above you and from below you, and behold, the eyes became dim and the hearts gaped up to the throats, and ye imagined various [vain] thoughts about Allah! In that situation the Believers were tried: they were shaken as by a tremendous shaking. And behold! The Hypocrites and those in whose hearts is a disease [even] say: 'Allah and His Messenger promised us nothing but delusion!' Behold! A party among them said: 'Oh men of Yathrib! Ye cannot stand [the attack]! therefore go back!' And a

band of them ask for leave of Muhammad, saying, 'Truly our houses are bare and exposed,' though they were not exposed they intended nothing but to run away. And if an entry had been affected to them from the sides [of the city], and they had been incited to sedition, they would certainly have brought it to pass, with none but a brief delay! ... They think that the Confederates have not withdrawn; and if the Confederates should come [again], they would wish they were in the deserts [wandering] among the Bedouins, and seeking news about you [from a safe distance]; and if they were in your midst, they would fight but little... When the Believers saw the Confederate forces, they said: 'This is what Allah and his Messenger had promised us, and Allah and His Messenger told us what was true.' And it only added to their faith and their zeal in obedience." (The Confederates:10-22)

4
The Conquest of Makkah
11 January 630 CE (10 Ramadan, 8 A.H.)

It was time to pray. Hadrat Bilal called the Adhan. Its sound rose towards the heavens as I held a cup of water in one hand and a date in the other, ready to break the fast.

This was the first week of Ramadan. The night was so majestic: the sky looked softer, like black velvet, with the crescent moon shining amongst the stars. We prayed the evening prayer with the Prophet ﷺ. Every word seemed like a jewel resting on my heart.

"Sit here, Abdul Karim!" my friend Abdul Wadud called out, as I joined the others for a group meal at the Mosque.

I greeted him with a smile. "*Alhamdulillah*, a blessed night," I said, as I surveyed the food offered: a meal of bread, dates and a stew made of goat meat. It looked delicious.

We were just finishing the meal when a commotion was heard outside the entrance to the Mosque. From the voices and the sounds, it seemed to be a large group of men arriving on horses.

Abdul Wadud and I exchanged nods, grabbed our swords and ran over to the Mosque's wide doorway, to see who it was and what their intentions were.

There were about forty men, dusty from the journey across the desert.

They dismounted from their horses and announced: "We are from the Bani Khuza, allied with the Prophet Muhammad! The Quraysh have broken the treaty; we ask an audience with the Prophet Muhammad, who swore we would have his allegiance."

A crowd had gathered by then. Abdul Wadud reassured them; "Indeed, you have allied yourself with the most trustworthy man in all Arabia – he is a man of his word. Come with us."

We led the men inside to where the Prophet ﷺ was eating with Abu Bakr ؓ, 'Ali ؓ and 'Umar ؓ. The Prophet ﷺ stood up and invited them to eat at their table, and to explain what happened. Abdul Wadud and I sat down nearby where we could listen.

After they helped themselves to the stew and bread, the leader began; "We are seeking justice according to the terms of the Treaty of Hudaybiyyah. Our enemies, the Bani Bakr, have killed our kinsmen in the sacred precincts of Makkah. They were helped by Ikrama and a few others of the Quraysh."

The killing of some of their tribe by the Bani Bakr, who were allied with the Quraysh, meant that the Treaty of Hudaybiyyah had been broken. Under the agreement, which the Quraysh and the Prophet ﷺ had signed about two years ago, the Prophet ﷺ agreed to not go to Makkah to perform the pilgrimage. In exchange, there would be a truce between the tribes; so if anyone attacked someone from either side, the treaty would be broken.

The Prophet ﷺ told them that the Quraysh needed to pay blood money to those who were killed and sever the allegiance between them and the Bani

Bakr. The Bani Khuza seemed happy with this decision.

A messenger was sent the next morning to inform the Quraysh and returned a week later. But instead of agreeing to the demands of paying the blood money and reinstating the treaty, the Quraysh said that the treaty was now invalid.

What does this mean? I thought to myself, considering the options. Now we could go to Makkah and perform Hajj, unhindered, with every right to do so. However, it also meant that a potential state of war was now between us.

Just as the news had fully spread around Medina, Abu Sufyan, the leader of the Quraysh, arrived in Medina. I found him wandering from door to door, trying to gain an audience with the Prophet ﷺ. He stopped me and asked, "Do you know who I am, boy?" Firstly, I didn't like him calling me 'boy', and secondly, I didn't really want to speak to him. He had the long robes of an important man of Makkah and had an arrogant yet desperate look on his face.

"I don't think I can help you," I said and backed away, bumping into Hadrat 'Umar, who was tall and fierce.

Hadrat 'Umar said, "Yes, we know you, Abu

Sufyan—the one who has brought suffering and difficulties to the Muslims! The one whose wife ate the liver of the Prophet's beloved uncle. Clear off back to Makkah!"

Abu Sufyan glared angrily, but did not reply as he hurriedly walked away.

Finally, Abu Sufyan went to the Prophet's ﷺ Mosque and announced, "The Treaty of Hudaybiyyah is reinstated!" He then left to return to Makkah.

Everyone just looked at each other, puzzled as to why he would say this, what was he so worried about?

We soon found out. After praying and seeking inspiration from Allah, the Prophet ﷺ announced that we would go to Makkah and restore peace and justice to the sacred city. "There is no other way to eradicate unbelief and draw a line for injustice, so let preparations for battle be made immediately."

Excited by the news, I went around the military camp area, preparing and helping where I could. Depending on how the conquest went, we could once and for all defeat the Quraysh and be able to visit the sacred Kaaba and perform Hajj.

Medina had been so busy in the last year. Many tribes from all over Arabia had come to give their oath of allegiance to the Holy Prophet Muhammad ﷺ: the Bani Sulaym, Bani Ghifar, Khuza'a, Bani Ka'b, Ashja to name but a few who until very recently, were bitter enemies of the Prophet ﷺ. We welcomed them all, finding accommodation for the many people. Abu Bakr, 'Umar and other merchants made sure a steady stream of supplies were coming into Medina to feed them.

The Prophet ﷺ would sit in the Mosque as they greeted him, one by one. His presence was like a shining star, emanating infinite wisdom, kindness and mercy, like a king in the Heavens but so humble on Earth. He always spent time with each and every one, listening until they had finished what they wished to say, and it made no difference if they were a leader of a tribe or a simple servant.

As I dropped off the last arrows and armor for repair, I listened as I walked through the groups of people. I heard these tribes' different dialects as I passed, intermixed with the noises of the goats and camels.

I had heard that the Prophet ﷺ was going to fast on the journey to Makkah, so that morning, I had woken early with 'Asma for my pre-dawn meal.

We had got married the year before. Whenever

I look back on the blessed event, my heart fills with happiness.

She has a beautiful soul, strong and passionate. She loves horses and is an excellent rider. I've been teaching her to use the bow and arrow and she is practicing shooting while riding her horse. She is also so kind and is always helping the poor and the needy. Soon we would be expecting our first baby, *insha'Allah*. We were still at my parents' house, Shukur had moved out to his own home a couple of years ago, so we had a room to ourselves.

My mother came down the stairs and saw me eating some soup. "You're not fasting on the journey to Makkah, are you? You know you don't do well in the heat. How will you keep up with the others?"

'Asma smiled to herself, finding this very amusing.

"Mother, I am not a child and I like to follow everything the Prophet does, if I can."

My mother gave me a worried look. "He also said you don't have to fast if you are on a journey."

"That is true, Mother," I said, not wanting to argue, "but do I have your permission?"

My mother looked away and thought for a moment and smiled at me. "I respect your choice—

and what better choice is there to follow in the Messenger of Allah's footsteps? May Allah make it easy for you." She gave me a hug and then sat down to have some bread and soup with us.

After saying goodbye to 'Asma and my mother, I went to the stables with my father to get our camels ready for the journey. I wished 'Asma could join me but she was pregnant so the harsh journey would be dangerous for her.

As I was putting the blanket on my camel, Khalid ibn Walid, a tall and intimidating warrior who had recently become Muslim, strode past me to find his horse which one of the finest black stallions at the stables.

"*As-salaamu 'alaikum*, Abdul Karim," he said as he passed.

A scene from the Battle of Uhud flashed across my mind; I had run down to collect the booty, deserting my brothers on the hill, then looked back to see Khalid and his troops kill them all in a surprise attack. As I looked at him my heart constricted, and anger rose up within me, my hand automatically went to my sword. My heart sensed though that he had changed and I relaxed my grip. I knew he had begged forgiveness from the Prophet, who had of course forgiven him.

He had promised he would work twice as hard to repair all the damage he had done.

My heart softened a bit and I calmed down. It was a great thing he was now on our side.

"*'Alaikum as-salaam*, Khalid, *alhamdulillah* you have joined us."

He smiled at me, perhaps he could sense my inner conflict and was aware some people might not be happy to see him as he had fought so hard against the Muslims.

It was time to find the Prophet ﷺ to receive his orders for the march to Makkah. My father and I led our camels through the streets with Khalid, who moved at quite a pace to where the Prophet ﷺ was organising the troops. I noticed the Prophet ﷺ was wearing a black turban, which he often wore to battles. He had the look of majesty about him. He greeted us as we arrived. He asked Khalid to organise an unruly bunch of Bedouins that had joined us. My father and I went with the *Ansar*.

I double-checked to see if my bag and provisions were well packed on the camel, as well as my armor and weapons. My best weapon was my bow and arrows, which were resting in the leather quiver my father had made me. The bow was skilfully crafted by a tribe north west of Medina; they used the finest wood and horse hair. Everything seemed secure so I mounted my camel and trotted over to join my brothers, beside whom I had fought at Badr. We were welcomed warmly.

"Ah, here comes Abdul Karim and Abdul Wadud. *As-salaamu 'alaikum!*"

"*Alaikum as-salaam!*" we both replied, happy to be with them.

Most of them were older men, similar in age to my father. I was one of the youngest to have fought at Badr.

We looked behind us at the incredible numbers of the various tribes as they were lining up to get ready for the march. I could not see the end of them, there were so many—perhaps as many as ten thousand men. This was unbelievable, *subhanAllah*. Only a few years ago there were just three hundred of us who fought at the Battle of Badr, a tiny group—but with the Creator of the Universe on our side.

Everything was ready – the camels were loaded up with supplies, the men mounted on horses or camels or walking on foot. The women and children called after us and sang for Allah's Glory and our success. Their voices faded into the distance as we headed towards Makkah, almost three hundred miles away.

The continual skyline of the jagged, grey rocks of the mountains rose up on either side of us. Underfoot, the road was gravelly. The landscape from Medina to Makkah consisted of rocks and large boulders. Occasionally a small dry tree poked out of the ground. I was used to the arid semi-desert, but after many hours of walking while fasting under the hot sun, I began to feel increasingly thirsty. My throat was dry as a bone and the desert seemed hazy. I would look over to the Prophet ﷺ now and then, but he seemed to not be affected by the fast.

A special strength kept us going, so we were able to make good time and rested at 'Usfan. I was so thirsty, feeling more and more desperate for some water. We sat near to the Prophet ﷺ, grateful for the rest.

The Prophet ﷺ then asked for a cup of water and broke his fast there, to show he would not be fasting more on this journey. Very relieved, we all followed suit and broke our fast. The Prophet ﷺ smiled at me. It showed to me again the mercy of Allah, who knows our every need.

I always tried to follow the example of the Prophet ﷺ and his family as much as I could, even though it was hard sometimes. I heard that 'Ali ؑ and the Prophet's ﷺ daughter Fatima ؑ so generously gave all of their food to the beggars if any came to their door. Once this happened three days in a row so they ended up fasting for three days with no food. Fatima ؓ said that after that, Allah had made it so that she never again felt the pangs of hunger.

We resumed our march, taking an unusual route to catch the Quraysh unaware. The day was cooler than usual and many hours later at dusk, we made camp near Makkah. Another two thousand warriors had joined us along the way, increasing our numbers to about twelve thousand.

When we reached a place called Marr al-Zahran, the Prophet ﷺ ordered us to make lots of fires, so that the whole valley was lit up. Thus, our numbers would seem vast and the Makkans would be encouraged to surrender peacefully. The Holy Prophet ﷺ never wanted to shed blood and if we could enter Makkah without a battle; then it would be a great triumph.

The next morning, we woke and prayed *Fajr* with the Holy Prophet ﷺ under the stars. His beautiful recitation of the Qur'an filled our hearts with inspiration and faith. Nothing else seemed to matter when I heard the Prophet ﷺ recite the Qur'an. When he recited *Surah Ya Siin* after the prayer, I wondered at the *Ayat*:

"It is not for the Sun to overtake the Moon, nor does the night outstrip the day. They all float, each in an orbit." (Ya-Siin:40)

I looked across the low mountains on the horizon as dawn was breaking and wondered if our Earth was also floating around the sun. *SubhanAllah*, each word carried oceans of meaning that only the heart could understand. The Heavens that morning seemed expectant of an impending great event.

As the sun rose higher and the radiant yellow light filled the pale blue sky, we moved off towards Makkah, each tribe forming different units: the Ghifar, Juhaina, the tribe of Saad bin Huzaim and Banu Sulaim, as well as the Ansar and the Companions of the Prophet ﷺ.

As we marched past, I saw the Prophet's ﷺ uncle, 'Abbas with Abu Sufyan, both of whom had arrived during the night. They were standing on a hillock, staring incredulously as they saw rank after rank of each tribe marching past them, the cries of, "*Allahu Akbar, Allahu Akbar!*" filling the valley. We were in the second-to-last contingent, led by Hadrat S'ad bin 'Umaidah.

The Prophet ﷺ said, "Today the Kaaba will be dressed in glory!"

The army was divided into four parts, each entering Makkah by its four gates. The Prophet ﷺ rode on his favorite camel, Al-Kaswa, with complete humility, his forehead almost touching the camel's back as he entered Makkah. As he rode, he recited *Surah Al Fath:*

"We have granted to you, [Muhammad] a manifest victory. That Allah may forgive your community their past faults and those to follow and complete His favor to you and keep you on a right way, and that Allah might help you with a mighty help. It is He who sent down tranquillity into the hearts of the believers that they would increase in faith along with their [present] faith. And to Allah belong the soldiers of the Heavens and the Earth, and ever is Allah Knowing and Wise." (The Victory:1-4)

A small band of warriors including Ikrama ibn Abu Jahl, Suhayl ibn 'Amr, and Safwan ibn Umayya attempted to attack Khalid's troops who were arriving from the north-east, through Khandama and Lait. After a brief fight, the Quraysh lost twelve men and we lost two of our warriors: Hubaish bin Al-Ashar and Kurz bin Jabir Al-Fihri, who returned to their Lord as Martyrs.

Besides this, there was little resistance. To my surprise, I had heard that Abu Sufyan had taken his *shahada* the night before and became Muslim. *Was this a sincere shahada?* I wondered.

Today he rode ahead of us and told the people what the Prophet ﷺ had said to him:

"Whoever enters the Mosque will be safe; whoever laid down his arms will be safe; whoever remains in his house and shuts the door and whoever is in the house of Abu Sufyan will be in safety."

As we walked peacefully through the streets of Makkah towards the Kaaba, we saw people peering out of their doors or from an upstairs window, fear and curiosity on their faces - perhaps they were not sure if Abu Sufyan's message was true?

As we approached the Kaaba itself, the Prophet ﷺ, after so many years and struggles, paused as he beheld it, and began to recite, "*Allahu Akbar!*" We all joined in and recited; "*Allahu Akbar! Allahu Akbar!*" The whole of Makkah, the Heavens and Earth were reverberating with our cries. Then the Prophet ﷺ asked for the key to the Kaaba.

The Prophet ﷺ went up to the door with the key and turned to face the crowd. Everyone became quiet to hear what the Prophet ﷺ would say. He called out, "O Quraysh, what do you expect from me today?"

And they said, "Mercy, O Prophet of Allah. We expect nothing but good from you."

The Prophet ﷺ replied, "Today I will speak to you as Yusuf spoke to his brothers. I will not harm you and Allah will forgive you, for He is Merciful and Loving. Go, you are free."

SubhanAllah, the breaths of relief were heard; such merciful words were not usual in these situations. All the torment, all the killings of Muslims, the perpetual harsh treatment, banishing the Prophet ﷺ to survive in the desert for years, killing many of his family. Even one of these things warranted harsh punishment, yet the Prophet ﷺ set everyone free. Again, my heart welled with love for Muhammad ﷺ. Has ever a man like him walked this Earth?

The Prophet ﷺ recited this *ayah* from the

Qur'an:

"No reproach this day shall be on you; Allah will forgive you; He is the Most Merciful of the Merciful." (Yusef: 92)

Some of the people began to cry out of relief and others simply dropped their swords in astonishment. The Prophet ﷺ and 'Ali went into the Kaaba.

While we waited until they came out, I remembered seeing the Kaaba many years ago, when my father used to come to Makkah to trade. As he carried out his business, I would sit by the side and look at the Kaaba. It was a tall, square building made of large stone blocks. I used to see the pagans walk around it, some with no clothes on, with animal skins over their shoulders and marks on their faces.

I went in once and saw all the idols. It smelt musty in there, with hundreds of different stone and wood faces looking at me. There were pictures of the Prophet Ibrahim عليهوسلم and Prophet Ismael عليهوسلم ; there were pictures of angels on the walls and a great stone statue of Hubal, the idol of Makkah. I had felt uncomfortable, like something was in there with them.

STORIES FROM THE BATTLES OF THE PROPHET MUHAMMAD ﷺ

Conquest of Makkah

THE CONQUEST OF MAKKAH

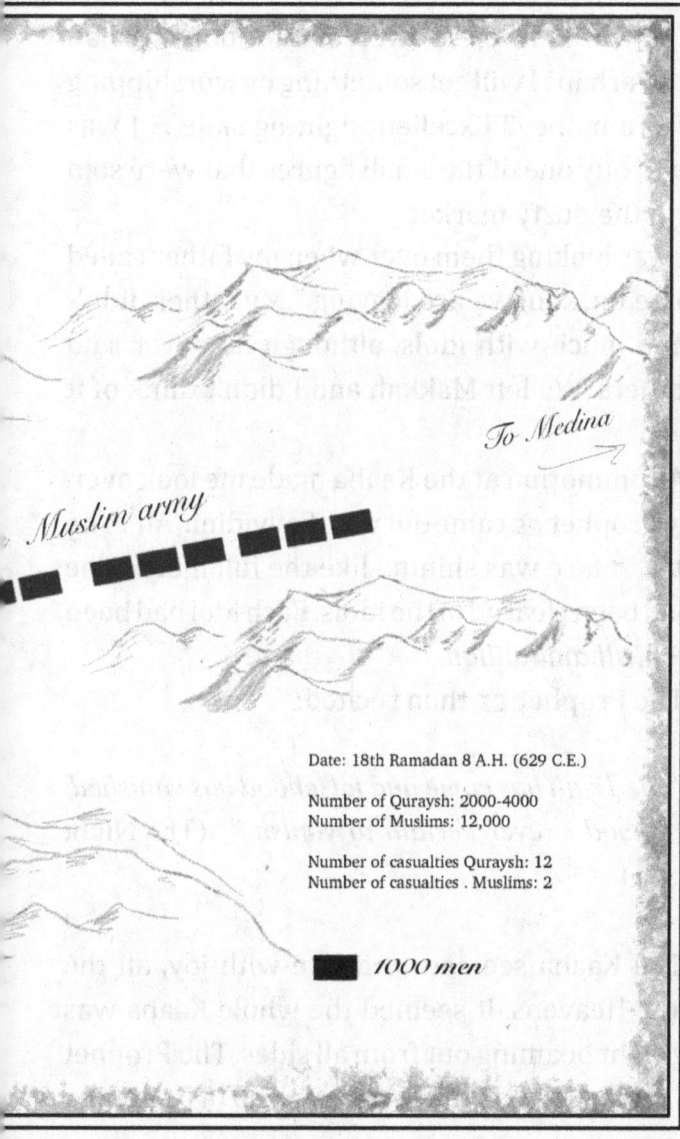

To Medina

Muslim army

Date: 18th Ramadan 8 A.H. (629 C.E.)

Number of Quraysh: 2000-4000
Number of Muslims: 12,000

Number of casualties Quraysh: 12
Number of casualties . Muslims: 2

■ *1000 men*

"Maybe it is the power of the idols?" I had thought. "Perhaps I will get something by worshipping them? More money? Excellent fighting skills?" I was tempted to buy one of the small figures that were sold outside in the dusty market.

I was looking them over when my father called out, "Come on, son, we are leaving." My father didn't bother too much with idols, although he never said that to others. We left Makkah and I didn't think of it again.

A commotion at the Kaaba made me look over. The Holy Prophet ﷺ came out with Sayyidina 'Ali. The Prophet's ﷺ face was shining like the full moon. The Kaaba had been cleared of the idols. Each idol had been destroyed, *alhamdulillah*.

The Prophet ﷺ then recited:

"The Truth has come and falsehood has vanished, truly falsehood is ever certain to vanish." (The Night Journey: 81)

The Kaaba seemed to dance with joy, all the way to the Heavens. It seemed the whole Kaaba was glowing, light beaming out from all sides. The Prophet ﷺ then began to circle the Kaaba with all of us joining him. As my feet walked on the dusty ground, circling the holiest place in the world, I felt a new feeling of contentment, joy and surrender to Allah. Heavenly blessings were streaming down, like cool water in the midday heat, and my soul felt entirely refreshed.

The Prophet ﷺ then gave a sermon to us all:

"*La ilaha il-Allah*. Idolatry is now abolished, no one is to worship any other man, or what is made of wood, stone or clay. Allah has made true His Promise. He has given support to His servant and has routed those who gathered against Him, wishing to extinguish the light of Islam. All the blood feuds and litigations of the time of ignorance are abolished. The only appointment to be upheld is the custodianship of the Holy Kaaba. And the distribution of water to the pilgrims. O people of Quraysh! Allah has lifted from you all the self-conceit from the age of ignorance, the vain glory of your predecessors, and your pride in the rotting bones of your ancestors. All of Mankind is descended from Adam, and Adam was created from clay. The Lord Almighty has made you male and female and divided you up into many people and tribes so that you might understand each other and live together as one spirit in a multitude of bodies."

Bilal climbed on top of the Kaaba and called the *adhan*, each word ringing out for all of Makkah to hear. *Allahu Akbar*! My joy was almost uncontainable.

The Prophet ﷺ said, "This was destined to be and it came to pass." He recited *Surah al-Fath* again—which was recommended to be recited on the first night of Ramadan – and said to everyone:

"Allah has made Makkah a sanctuary since the day He created the Heavens and the Earth, and it will remain a sanctuary by virtue of the sanctity Allah has bestowed on it till the Day of Resurrection. [Fighting in] it was not made lawful to anyone before me, nor will it be made lawful to anyone after me, and it was not made lawful for me except for a short period of time. Its game should not be chased, nor should its trees be cut, nor its vegetation or grass uprooted, not its *Luqata* (lost things) picked up except by one who makes a public announcement about it."

The Messenger of Allah ﷺ then went up the Safa hill and accepted the allegiance of the Quraysh. This was the same place, almost twenty years ago, that he had first declared his prophethood, but was harshly rejected. Now, he was accepting allegiance to Islam from thousands of people on the very same hill.

We stayed eighteen days in Makkah before

returning to Medina. During that time the Prophet ﷺ ordered the Kaaba to be covered with red and white-striped Yemeni cloth. This was the first time the Kaaba was covered, and it looked so majestic, *mashAllah*.

Sayyidina 'Ali told us what happened inside the Kaaba when he and the Prophet ﷺ went in to remove the idols. There were some high up on the walls which they could not reach so he offered to let the Prophet ﷺ stand on his shoulders to remove them. The Prophet ﷺ had smiled and told him, "You cannot carry me, but you can stand on my shoulders."

When he stood on the Prophet's ﷺ shoulders, he saw a most wondrous spiritual vision: the Divine Throne. He saw that the head of the Prophet ﷺ covered the Throne, his chest filled the heavenly worlds and then the Earth was covered by his blessed feet.

After the conquest of Makkah, there just remained the town of Tai'f, west of Makkah. They had assumed the Prophet Muhammad ﷺ would come and take revenge after their bad treatment of him—chasing him away; throwing stones at him after he was banished from Makkah—and was seeking shelter. Instead of waiting to see what happened, we heard they were getting ready to attack.

We marched over there and fought them at Hunain, a narrow pass before Tai'f, where seventy of their number fell but only four Muslims were martyred. After a siege of many days, the rest were all taken prisoner, but the Prophet ﷺ released them soon after, such was his mercy. He also gave gifts to various people amongst them.

Six months later, the chief of Tai'f arrived in Medina to take his *shahada* and countless more people arrived from far and wide to take allegiance to the Messenger of Allah ﷺ, declaring their Islam.

"When comes the Help of Allah [to you, O Muhammad] against your enemies and the conquest [of Makkah], And you see that the people enter Allah's religion [(Islam] in crowds, So glorify the Praises of your Lord, and ask for His Forgiveness. Verily, He is the One Who accepts the repentance and forgives. The Divine Support 110:1-3)

THE CONQUEST OF MAKKAH

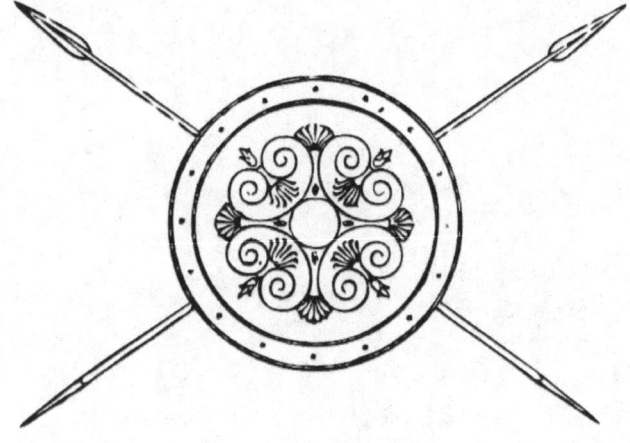

Rules of Battle in Islam

War is an unpleasant fact of life, which seems to persist throughout all times in history. Islam is unique in that it recognises this unfortunate situation and is able to set codes of conduct in battle for those times when there is no other choice. Thanks to the efforts of the early Muslims engaging in battle, there are clear rules that protect innocent lives and maintain acceptable standards.

The Prophet ﷺ only engaged in battle when:

- ✥ A clan or group did not respond to diplomacy or listened to reason.
- ✥ A clan or group was intent on destroying Islam.
- ✥ A clan or group was intent on fighting.
- ✥ A clan or group committed an act of treachery.

If a battle had to take place, then the following rules apply:
- "Do not kill any child, any woman, or any elder or sick person." (*Sunan Abu Dawud*)

- "Do not practice treachery or mutilation." (*Al-Muwatta*)

- "Do not uproot or burn palms or cut down fruitful trees." (*Al-Muwatta*)

- "Do not slaughter a sheep or a cow or a camel, except for food." (*Al-Muwatta*)

- "If one fights his brother, [he must] avoid striking the face, for God created him in the image of Adam." (*Bukhari & Muslim*)

- "Do not kill the monks in monasteries, and do not kill those sitting in places of worship." (*Musnad Ahmad Ibn Hanbal*)

- "Do not destroy the villages and towns, do not spoil the cultivated fields and gardens, and do not slaughter the cattle." (*Sahih Bukhari*)

- "Do not wish for an encounter with the enemy; pray to God to grant you security; but when you [are forced to] encounter them, exercise patience." (*Sahih Muslim*)

- "No one may punish with fire except the Lord of fire." (*Sunan Abu Dawud*)

- "Do not kill the workers/wage earners [ie those workers not fighting you.]" (*Ahmad*)

- Violations against women are also prohibited. This is covered in the general laws of the Shariah as being illegal and against the Divine and moral law and war does not provide an exception.

- Actions such as suicide bombing, killing unarmed civilians and fighting without permission in rebel groups is all against the way of the Prophet ﷺ and unlawful in Islam. (From Sheikh Muhammad Hisham Kabbani's ق fatwa 2013)

Notes

I wish to thank the authors of three books in particular who inspired these stories: Hajja Amina Adil ق, the wife of the great saint, Sheikh Nazim al-Haqqani ق, Sheikh Hisham Kabbani ق and Sayyid Ameenul Hassan Rizvi. I would also like to thank Hana for all her support and Rose McBride.

There are a great many hadiths about these battles, some of which have slightly contradictory statements, but have been put together by scholars over the years to form the general narrative we hear in these stories. I have not changed any of the key events or actual quotes from the Holy Prophet ﷺ but have kept them to be as accurate as possible in accordance with established *Seera* of the Prophet ﷺ. May Allah forgive any inaccuracies or assumptions that I have unintentionally made.

The Prophet's ﷺ life story is told generation after generation, teaching people through the events that are preserved from that time. Everyone's life is a drama in itself but this story and the events that unfolded are a mighty allegory for the development of faith.

This story unfolds with the different personalities representing different sides to the self. The Holy Prophet ﷺ represents perfection, enlightenment and guidance. Abu Jahl, and the other leaders of the Quraysh, the bitter enemy; striving to destroy belief and guidance.

It's a story of the eventual triumph of light over darkness, so that the whole of Arabia, representing the whole of the self, turns to Islam and is forgiven by Allah.

"The Truth has come and falsehood has vanished, truly falsehood is ever certain to vanish." (The Night Journey: 81)

May Allah guide our ways to Him and forgive us and Allah knows best in all things. *Ameen*

Symbols and Translations

Symbols

Traditionally in Islam, phrases of respect are added after mentioning Allah , the Prophet Muhammad ﷺ, the other prophets, the Prophet's ﷺ Companions and the Saints. For authenticity, common Arabic words and phrases have also been used.

ﷻ	*Jalla jalaluhu*: "May his Glory be glorified."
ﷺ	*Sallahu alayhi wa salaam*: "Peace and blessing be upon him.
عليهوسلم	*Alayhi salaam*: "Peace be upon them."
	Radhiya llahu anhu: "Well-pleased is Allah with them."
ق	*Qaddas-Allahu sirrah*: "May God sanctify their secret."

Translations

'Alaikum as-salaam	"And peace and blessings to you."
Adhan	The call to prayer
Alhamdulillah	"All praise belongs to God."
Allah	God's Name
Allahu Akbar	"God is the greatest."

The Ansar	The 'Helpers' of Medina who shared their homes and provision with the migrating Muslims from Makkah.
As-salaamu 'alaikum	"Peace and blessings be upon you."
Ayat	Verse from Qur'an
Bismillahirrahmanirrahim	"In the Name of Allah, the most Compassionate and the most Merciful."
Dhikr	Remembrance of Allah.
Dhuhr and Asr	Two of the five daily prayers.
Insha'Allah	"If Allah Wills it"
Jumu`ah	The Friday congregational prayer.
La ilaha il-Allah	"There is no god except Allah."
RasoolAllah	Messenger of Allah
Shahada	Bearing witness that: 'There is no God but Allah and Muhammad is the Messenger of Allah.'
SubhanAllah	"Glory belongs to Allah."
Wu'du	Ritual Ablution

References and Further Reading

The Messenger of Allah by Hajja Amina Adil, published by The Islamic Supreme Council of America, 2002

Battles by the Prophet, in the Light of the Qur'an by Sayyid Ammenul Hasan Rizvi, published by S. Abdul Majeed & Co., Malaysia, 1997

Jihad by Sheikh Hisham Kabbani, published by The Islamic Supreme Council of America 2010

Sahih al Bukhari, published by Darussalam, Saudi Arabia, 1997

Muhammad Messenger of Allah Ash-Shifa of Qadi 'Iyad, translated by Aisha Abdul Rahman Bewley, Medina Press 1991

Men Around the Messenger by Khalid Muhammad Khalid, Al Manara Press,

Find out other Islamic educational books by Halima Publishing!

Science in the Qur'an - Comparing the ancient verses with modern scientific discoveries.

ISBN 9781999802707

A Young Person's Guide to Islamic History - Book 1 -The True Story of Jihad in the Life of the Prophet Muhammad ﷺ.

ISBN - 9781999802776

A Young Person's Guide to Islamic History - Book 2 - The Rashidun Khulafah.
ISBN - 9781999802745

www.ingramcontent.com/pod-product-compliance
Lightning Source LLC
Chambersburg PA
CBHW011406070526
44577CB00003B/395